PRESENTED TO

_____

BY

_____

ON THE OCCASION OF

_____

DATE

_____

All that I am or hope to be,
I owe to my mother.

ABRAHAM LINCOLN

MOTHERING by HEART

Celebrating the Moments that Last Forever

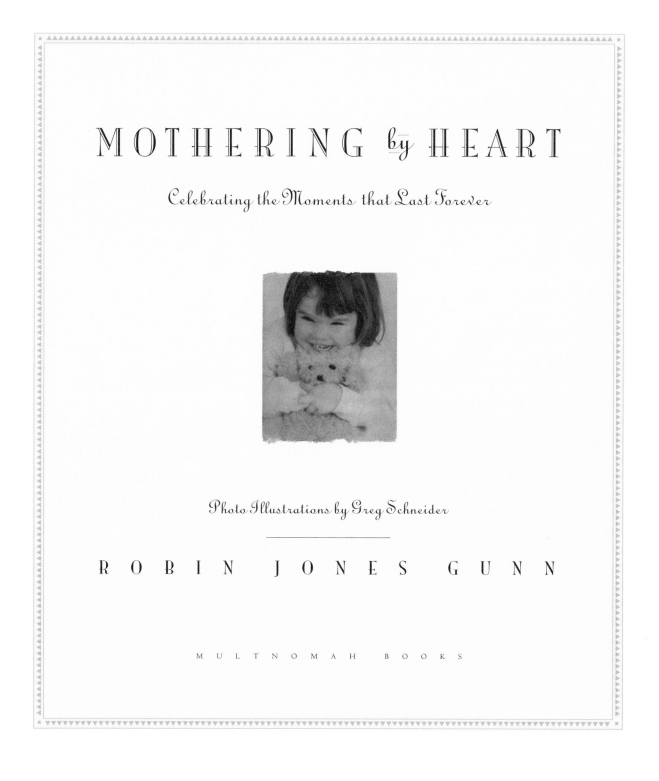

Photo Illustrations by Greg Schneider

ROBIN JONES GUNN

MULTNOMAH BOOKS

MOTHERING BY HEART

published by Multnomah Books, a part of the Questar publishing family

© 1996 by Robin Jones Gunn
Illustrations ©1996 by Greg Schneider
Designed by David Uttley
International Standard Book Number: 0-88070-888-3

Printed in the United States of America

Most Scripture quotations are from:
The New King James Version (NKJV) © 1984 by Thomas Nelson, Inc.
The Message, ©1994 by Eugene Peterson, NavPress

For information:
QUESTAR PUBLISHERS, INC.
POST OFFICE BOX 1720
SISTERS, OREGON 97759

96 97 98 99 00 01 02 03 — 10 9 8 7 6 5 4 3 2 1

C O N T E N T S

Sometimes We Had to Laugh

You Made Each Day a Miracle

Didn't You Grow Too Fast?

MOTHERING BY HEART

My husband, Ross, and I sat silently in the doctor's office. Ross reached over and took my hand in his. The doctor bustled in the door, positioned himself behind his great mahogany desk and said, "Your suspicions were correct. You are pregnant."

From that very moment, I felt changed. No longer just a woman, just a daughter, or just a wife; I was a mother. Entrusted by God to do that which is not gifted to men or even to angels. Only a woman's body can carry and nurture new life.

During the months that followed, I was constantly amazed. I understood why Hannah cried out to the Lord; I could see how Sarah's first reaction was to laugh. And as the baby "leaped" inside

me, I shared the joy Elizabeth must have felt.

When our son was born, I followed Mary's example of watching the miracle unfold and pondering all these things in my heart. My journal became like a wicker basket slung over my arm as I ventured into the woods of Motherhood.

For more than a decade I collected treasures of childhood innocence, glimpses of the eternal, and moments of private wonder. Our two children, Ross IV ("Young Ross") and Rachel Elizabeth, filled that basket, as all children do.

Here is a handful of those remembrances. A sharing of secrets. An invitation to come and spend a few quiet moments reminiscing with a kindred heart.

- Robin Jones Gunn

You made all the delicate,
inner parts of my body
and knit them together
in my mother's womb.

PSALM 139:13
LIVING BIBLE

THE FIRST TIME I SAW YOU

Pink flesh pressed against my cheek,
Tiny fingers curled up tight,
Gentle coos of such delight—
It is no secret:
You've captured my heart.

I will wait on the Lord…
And I will hope in Him.
Here am I and the children whom
the Lord has given me!

ISAIAH 8:17-18 (NKJV)

Waiting

Dear Baby, here beneath my heart,
I thought that you might come today;
the timing just seemed right.

But the stars are out
and the moon is high
and sheepishly I wonder why
I try to arrange the plans
of God.

For now I know
you will not come
until the One who holds eternity
rustles your soft cocoon and
whispers in tones that I will not hear,
"It's time, precious gift.

"Now it's time."

During the first weeks
I used to lie long hours with the baby in my arms,
watching her sleep,
sometimes catching a gaze from her eyes:
feeling very near the edge,
the mystery,
perhaps the knowledge of life.

ISADORA DUNCAN
1878-1927

TENDER INTUITION

I hold you in my arms, young prince. You sleep in sweet, heavenly peace. Yet, I wonder if you'd be so calm if you knew the truth: I am your mother. And I don't have the slightest idea what I'm doing. You are my first baby ever. My only son. I was just getting used to being pregnant, and now here you are! And you are so very, very real.

I've been preparing for your arrival for months. I've read the books. Well, some of them. A few pages. I've listened to my friends who give me endless advice. They're all experienced, you know, because they have their own babies. But you're different. You're my baby. And they don't know a thing about you.

I do. I know all about the way you kick and wiggle. I've already memorized the way you smell, like a fresh-from-the-earth daffodil. I know about the way your lower lip quivers when you're about to cry. I know that your wispy hair is the most luxuriously soft thing that has ever touched my cheek.

Yet I admit, there's much I don't know. In the hospital I had to be instructed on how to nurse you. Yesterday my mother showed me how to bathe you in the sink. I don't have a clue how to clear up diaper rash. I get queasy at the sight of blood. I don't sew. I'm not good at salt dough maps. My math skills are atrocious. And you might as well know right up—that wiggly teeth give me the heebie-jeebies.

However, I am very good at baking cookies. I know how to make indoor tents on rainy days. And I have my father's wonderful sense of humor so I

know how to laugh and how to make you laugh.

I'll sing you sweet songs in the night. I'll pray for you every day. I'll let you keep any animal you catch, as long as you can feed it. I'll call all your imaginary friends by their first names. I'll put love notes in your lunch box, and I'll swim with you in the ocean, even when I'm old.

Perhaps my best qualification to be your mother is that I share this privilege with the most incredible man in the world—your father.

Such secrets of motherhood can't be learned over coffee with friends. They can't be taught by a book, or even by trial and error. To me, these are tender intuitions what matter most. Eternal insights only a mother can know—when her baby is in her arms as you are now in mine. This is where the Lord will teach me how to mother you by heart.

FOR RACHEL

Rachel Elizabeth,

Little Lamb, Gift of God,

You came into this world so fast and furious!

One moment I was gasping for air.

The next I pried my eyes open and greeted

your lizard-like pose upon my chest.

Imagine!

You were just born and already you

held your head up,

blinking your eyes in the brightness.

I reached my heavier-than-lead arms

to touch you and

your still-wet, trembling hand

clasped my eager finger.

Then you curled up into a ten-pound ball

of wailing flesh.

Today, at eighteen months,

you still come at me hard and fast.

I close my eyes for one moment

and there you are—

on top of the table, out the front door.

I'm exhausted

from monitoring your independence.

Such strength. Such determination.

Then comes a night like tonight

when you fight sleep,

holding up that stiff neck so assuredly

until at last, in my arms, you yield,

a twenty-pound ball of helpless flesh.

My snugly little lamb,

I smile at the future

for I know the Good Shepherd,

I hear His voice.

He makes you to lie down in flannel crib sheets.

He restores my soul.

Surely goodness and mercy will follow us

all the days of our lives.

Holy Sabbath

This Lord's Day,
I arose at six
prayed
showered
nursed the baby
fixed breakfast
dressed
ironed my husband's shirt
bathed the baby
dressed the baby
found my husband's watch
curled my hair
changed the baby's diaper
answered the phone
put on some makeup
stuck a roast in the oven
packed the diaper bag

grabbed my Bible
dashed to the kitchen for Linda's
casserole dish
ran to the car
and as I strapped my little angel
into his car seat
he vomited all over everything,
including me
and my only ironed dress.

Oh yes, Lord,
I shall remember this
Sabbath Day.
However, I must confess,
I am completely stumped
on how
to keep it holy.

Hush! my dear, lie still and slumber,
Holy angels guard thy bed!
Heavenly blessings without number
Gently falling on thy head.

How much better thou'rt attended
Than the Son of God could be,
When from heaven He descended
And became a child like thee!

May'st thou live to know and fear Him,
Trust and love Him all thy days;
Then go dwell forever near Him
See His face, and sing His praise.

ISAAC WATTS
1709

Early, Early Morning

It was early,

early morning.

That delicate time of day just before dawn

when it seems as if all creation is asleep.

In the cool,

gray light she gazed at the infant

sleeping in her arms.

Less than an hour old,

this tiny miracle shone perfect in every way.

She drew him close to feel the rhythm

of his steady heart beating against her skin.

A tear fell from her eye

and rolled across his cheek.

And with the tear came the memories.

How amazed she was the day

she found out she was pregnant!

How exhilarated and yet,

how terrified.

Trying to justify her condition

to her parents proved difficult,

to say the least.

More excruciating was the moment she

stood guileless

before the man she loved,

the man she planned to marry.

She found no words to make him

understand the awful truth:

The baby she carried was not his child.

She left home.

A gracious cousin took her in.

There she waited,

watching her body transform from girl to

woman as the life within her grew.

Was it a miracle

when her boyfriend had a change of heart

and took her back?

Was she the only one surprised when he said

he still wanted to marry her?

They left their small town together

as husband and wife,

with her due date rapidly approaching.

Then her contractions began—

tightening her abdomen with a force

more intense than she imagined

she could withstand.

Breathing hard,

she labored long into the night.

Finally

the urge to push overwhelmed her young body,

and the baby came.

Nothing of the past mattered anymore.

He was finally here!

Naked, exhausted, quivering in her arms.

Now,

as the first silver streaks of morning

pierced through the cracks in the stable,

she carefully, tenderly,

wrapped him in swaddling clothes

and laid him in the manger.

OFTEN YOU LED THE WAY

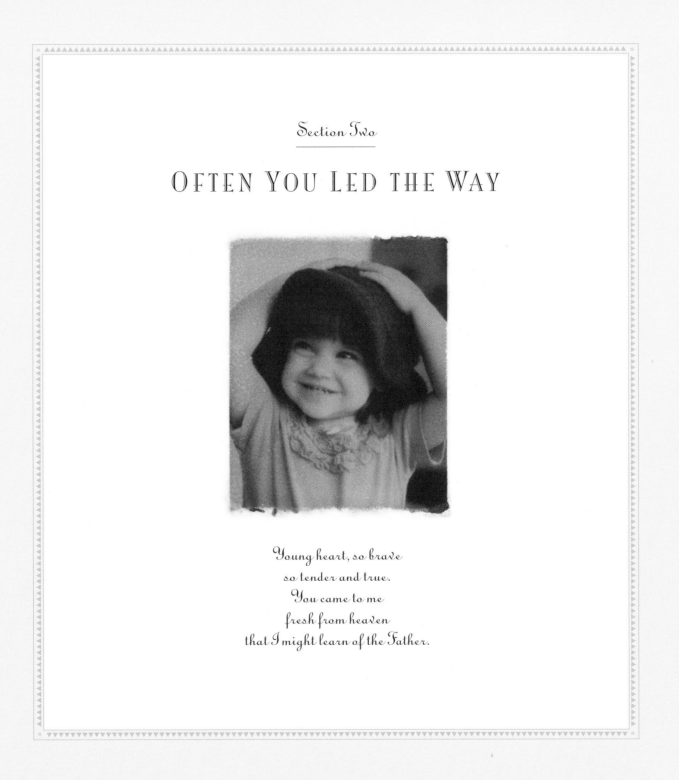

Young heart, so brave
so tender and true.
You came to me
fresh from heaven
that I might learn of the Father.

Thank you,
my little ones, for bringing with you
tender hearts and innocent eyes.

I love the way
you sprinkle your contagious giggles
all over my life.

SURRENDER

oday as we left the baseball field after Young Ross's Little League practice, he and Rachel ran to the playground. I watched Ross steady Rachel's three-year-old legs as she climbed up the steps on the slide. He told her to wait while he ran around to the front. Then he opened his arms to catch her. I was impressed. Such a courteous young man. So considerate. So thoughtful. For a brief moment, I thought of how easy this motherhood thing was and patted myself on the back for raising two such delightful children.

Then a round girl with dark hair in braids entered the sandy play area and headed for the slide. "Hey, I know you," my charming young man said. "Your mother works in the cafeteria at school."

The girl nodded shyly.

"Your mother is fat and ugly!" he said.

I froze. How could my own flesh and blood say such a thing!

The girl retaliated with, "Oh yeah? Your mother is fat and ugly, too!" Then she noticed me and meekly said, "Oh. I didn't mean it."

I waited for my son to apologize to her. But he didn't. I reacted. I scooped up Rachel and told Ross we were going to the car. He could join us after he apologized. I'd show him he most certainly could not get away with this "sin" of rudeness. Sin separates us from God, and now this belligerent seven-year-old's sin would separate him from me!

I marched off in a huff. Young Ross ran after me screaming, "Mommy, don't leave me!"

A man in his driveway rolled out from under his car, wrench in hand. He looked at me as if I

were a child-beater. I calmly unlocked the car doors and settled Rachel in the front seat. Young Ross had caught up and was wailing, "Mommy, what did I do?"

The mechanic's wife had now joined him in the driveway. Two other neighbors appeared across the street, and a boy on a bike pedaled our way to see what was going on. I motioned serenely for Young Ross to climb into the backseat.

I didn't close the door and drive off; I was afraid of what our audience might think of me. The tears streamed down my son's face; yet I believed it was important that I show what a fine mother I was. I would bring this situation under control, and we would all leave smiling, like a happy little Christian family, displaying our spotless testimony.

Calmly, I explained that it was rude to say the

girl's mother was fat and ugly. "But she is!" Young Ross replied innocently. I told him that God made that little girl's mommy and when Ross made fun of her, he was actually making fun of something God made. Couldn't he see how that would make God sad, being rude like that?

His expression went from painful wincing to terrified sobriety. I was pleased with myself for clearing things up so easily, and I might add, spiritually. His humility was instant. Now we could leave.

Before I could close the door, Young Ross said, "Mommy, we need to pray." I told him we would when we got home. No, he said, we had to pray right then and there, and he proceeded to climb out of the car and kneel on the muddy curb.

I was acutely aware of the half-dozen people who were now watching. Rachel stood on the front seat, her big, round eyes peering over the headrest. Young Ross waited for me to join him on the muddy curb. Hands folded, honest eyes staring up at me, he expected me to kneel beside him.

Suddenly I understood what this was all about. This wasn't about my son and his "sin" of rude-ness. This was about me and about my always needing to be right, to be in control. It was about my pride. My stubbornness. My sin.

I surrendered then. I had to. Down I went in front of God and the whole world. The mud felt cold on my knees.

I listened as my only son climbed up into the lap of our heavenly Father and told Him he was sorry and promised never again to make fun of anything God made. Then without questioning instant forgiveness, Young Ross opened his eyes, bounded out of the throne room and hopped into the car.

I stayed frozen on that curb another few, eternal seconds, whispering my prayer. When I rose and found my way to the driver's side of the car, I was trembling inside and out.

Our curious audience continued to stare. I'm sure we were quite a spectacle. But I didn't care. Let them stare. Let little girls call me fat and ugly. Let my jeans get muddied knees. But, oh, Father, never let me become too proud to surrender as a child before you.

PERFECT MOTHER

You mothers
have a habit of blaming yourself
for everything that goes wrong.
You were so determined to get it right —
to bring us up perfectly.

You forget. There's never a rehearsal.
For every child is totally unlike the others.

Of course you made mistakes.
But I don't want a Perfect Mother.

I want one who is human and can understand —
and lets me make my own catastrophes.

You haven't feet of clay —
Just ordinary human feet
subject to callouses and fallen arches.

I love you exactly as you are.

PAM BROWN
1928

Love Letters

One Sunday during the church service, Rachel sat next to me busily drawing on the back of an attendance card. She tugged on my sleeve and whispered could she please have a piece of very nice paper. I found in the back of my Bible a blank side of a hot pink bulletin insert. She was delighted.

I turned my attention back to the sermon and didn't look at her for a few minutes. When I did, she was sitting completely still, with the paper and pencil balanced perfectly on her lap, her hands at her side. She was staring straight ahead, as if purposely not looking at the paper.

I was about to ask if she was okay, but then I noticed what she had written in her eight-year-old penmanship. The note read, "Do yu LOVE me? Yes No." I'd seen these questions of hers before. She wanted the answer circled, either yes or no.

I smiled and reached for the pencil to draw a big happy circle around the Yes. But she unfroze and snatched the pencil away from me. "I didn't write it to you," she whispered. I glanced at the person on the other side of her. I didn't know the woman. I doubted Rachel did.

"Who *did* you write it to?"

"God."

She placed the pencil back on the paper and waited without moving a muscle.

I smiled and reached for the pencil to draw a big happy circle around the Yes.

All your children shall be taught by the Lord,
And great shall be the peace
of your children.

ISAIAH 54:13 (NKJV)

A BROTHER'S PRAYER

We ate outside one summer night on the back patio to enjoy the cool of the evening. I lifted Rachel out of her highchair so she and Young Ross could run barefoot in the grass. Ross and I sat and watched our kindergartner son being shadowed by his faithful sidekick, Rachel the Wonder Two-Year-Old. She followed him underneath the overturned plastic wading pool. A moment later, the green, belly-up pool began to scoot around the yard, propelled by four arms and four legs. Rachel's giggly voice called out, "It's cwazy twertle!"

We laughed. The pool stopped moving. We could hear the kids talking under their green dome, and we went back to our own conversation. A few minutes later Young Ross and Rachel popped up and rushed over to the table.

Young Ross said, "Go ahead, Rachel, tell them."

We waited.

Rachel laced her pudgy little fingers together and squeezed her eyes shut tight. "Dwr Desus."

"That's wonderful! Your big brother taught you how to pray, didn't he?"

She opened her bright baby blues and nodded.

Cool, calm brother said, "Yeah, but she doesn't say all the words right, so I just went ahead and asked Jesus into her heart for her."

"Yeah, but she doesn't say all the words right, so I just went ahead and asked Jesus into her heart for her."

Then they brought young children to Him,
that He might touch them;
but the disciples rebuked those who brought them.
But when Jesus saw it,
He was greatly displeased and said to them,
"Let the little children come to Me,
and do not forbid them;
for of such is the kingdom of God.

"Assuredly, I say to you,
whoever does not receive the kingdom of God
as a little child will by no means enter it."
And He took them up in His arms, put His hands on them,
and blessed them.

MARK 10:13-16 (NKJV)

TODDLERS IN EDEN

This morning from the upstairs nursery window I listened to my four-year-old son and his little friend Asenath. After playing in the sandbox, they were nestled together in the hammock, discussing what to play next.

Young Ross said he wanted to play Adam and Eve.

Asenath said no.

My son persisted, promising her it would be fun. He would be Adam, and she could be Eve.

No, Asenath didn't want to be Eve.

Young Ross asked, then who did she want to be?

Flipping back her golden curls she said, "I want to be God."

My son-of-a-Gunn said, "Hey! That's just what the snake said! You can be the snake!"

My son persisted, promising her it would be fun. He would be Adam, and she could be Eve.

AUTUMN DANCE

She stood a short distance from her guardian at the park this afternoon, her distinctive features revealing that although her body blossomed into young adulthood, her mind would always remain a child's. My children ran and jumped and sifted sand through perfect, coordinated fingers. Caught up in fighting over a shovel, they didn't notice when the wind changed. But she did. A wild autumn wind spinning the leaves into amber flurries. ❧ I called to my boisterous son and jostled my daughter. Time to go. Mom still has lots to do today. My rosy-cheeked boy stood still, watching with wide-eyed fascination the gyrating dance of the Down syndrome girl as she scooped up leaves and showered herself with a twirling rain of autumn jubilation. ❧ With each twist and hop she sang deep, earthy grunts—a canticle of praise meant only for the One whose breath causes the leaves to tremble from the trees. ❧ Hurry up. Let's go. Seat belts on? I start the car. In the rearview mirror I study her one more time through misty eyes. And then the tears come. Not tears of pity for her. The tears are for me. For I am too busy to dance in the autumn leaves and far too sophisticated to publicly shout praises to my Creator. ❧ I am whole and intelligent and normal, and so I weep because I will never know the severe mercy that frees such a child and bids her come dance in the autumn leaves.

At church today I watched a daddy lift his son
to the wooden offering box.
The toddler leaned over and deposited
a fistful of change.
Straight blond hair in a bowl cut,
clear blue eyes, the toddler reminded me
of Young Ross at that age.

PURE IN HEART

The boy turned to his daddy and asked,
"Is all this money for God?" Yes, it was, the father said.
The dad headed for the sanctuary.
The rascal in his arms wiggled and squealed,
"No, Daddy! Don't go yet! Wait there."
He pointed back at the offering box.
"I want to wait so I can see God when He comes
to get His money."

Real Treasure

"Do you see my concern?" the teacher asked, her arms folded across her chest.

We went to Open House tonight at the public elementary school. When Rachel's teacher met us, her eyebrows seemed to elevate slightly. She spoke kindly of our first grader but said she had some concerns. She then invited us to look at the artwork; we would see what she meant.

Dozens of brown paper treasure chests were tacked to the bulletin board. Each had a barreled top attached with a brad. On the front was printed, "A Real Treasure Would Be".…We walked over and began opening the lids to find Rachel's treasure and see why it so concerned the teacher.

As we peeked into each chest, we saw TVs and Nintendos, a few genies, heaps of gold coins, and a unicorn. Rachel's chest was in the very bottom corner. We had to stoop to open it. Inside, our daughter had drawn Christ, hanging on a cross with red drops of blood shaped like hearts dripping from his hands. She had completed the sentence, "A Real Treasure Would Be…Jesus."

"Do you see my concern?" the teacher asked, her arms folded across her chest.

"Yes," my husband agreed, "I see what you mean. The J is backwards, isn't it?"

True, a mother has many cares
but they are sweet cares.

JULIETTE MONTAGUE COOKE
1812

INNOCENT PETITIONS

When we lived in Reno, Rachel had a best friend named Kristin. We moved to Portland only a few days before Rachel's first day of second grade. Each night we talked about her new school and prayed together before she went to bed. The night before school started Rachel prayed that Jesus would give her a new best friend at this school and that her name would be Kristin. I felt compelled to alter her prayer but decided to let it go. How do I tell my child she shouldn't be so specific with God?

The next morning Rachel stood in front of the mirror while I combed her hair. She seemed lost in thought, and then suddenly she announced to me that Jesus was going to give her a new best friend. Her name would be Kristin, and she would have brown hair, just like the Kristin in Reno.

I quickly ran through all my mental notes on prayer. What would be the best way to explain to this child that prayer is not telling God what we have in mind for Him to do, but rather seeking His mind? I tried a few flimsy sentences. All fell flat. She seemed undaunted. I drove her to school still unable to find a way to protect her from her own prayer. I was afraid she would experience a spiritual crisis when she arrived at school and found no brunette Kristin in her class. What would that do to her innocent faith?

We entered the classroom, and Rachel found her name on her new desk. She lifted the top and began to examine the contents. I sat down at the desk next to hers and decided this would be a good time to explain how praying isn't like wishing.

It's not magic. You can't ask God for something and expect it to materialize at your command. She needed to be willing to accept whatever new friends God brought to her.

I was about to plunge in, when out of the corner of my eye I noticed the name of the student who would occupy the desk next to Rachel. There, in bold black letters, was printed Kristin.

I could barely speak. "Rachel," I finally managed in a whisper, "look! There *is* a Kristin in your class. And she's going to sit right next to you!"

"I know, Mom. She's the one I prayed for."

The bell rang, and I practically staggered to the back of the classroom as the students began to come in. Rachel sat up straight, folded her hands on her desk, and grinned confidently.

I glued my eyes to that door. Four boys entered. Then a girl with blond hair who took a seat in the first row. Two more boys and then, there she was! She sauntered shyly to the "Kristin" desk, caught Rachel's welcoming grin, and returned the same.

I probably don't need to mention that she had brown hair — down to her waist.

Or that everything I really need to know about prayer I learned in second grade.

Faith
brings us on highways
that make our reasoning dizzy.
CORRIE TEN BOOM

SOMETIMES WE HAD TO LAUGH

You surprise me.
You amaze me!
You razzle, dazzle, frazzle me!
And the only sure cure to get me by
is if I laugh until I cry.

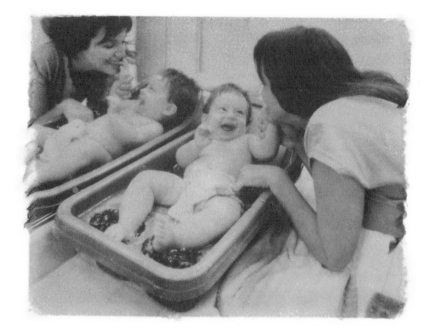

PAINTED ON THE WALL OF A CHURCH NURSERY
WHERE OUR BABIES ONCE VISITED:

Behold, I tell you a mystery:
We shall not all sleep,
but we shall all be changed.

1 CORINTHIANS 15:51 (NKJV)

MAYBE GOD LAUGHS

Yesterday Young Ross drew a special picture for Papa and Nana and found an envelope in the desk drawer. I caught him heading out the door with the bulky envelope clasped in his three-year-old fist.

I asked where he was going, and he said, "I go mailbox."

I told him he needed an address. The letter wouldn't get to Papa and Nana without an address. I told him to wait and I'd find the address for him right after lunch.

He handed me the envelope and scampered down the hall toward the bedrooms. I returned to the kitchen wondering why he had so willingly turned over the letter. I decided it must be because of my clear explanation. That's all a kid needs. A little understanding, a little explanation about how letters must have addresses before they can be mailed . . .

CRASH!

I ran to my bedroom and found him sprawled on the floor by the closet. Several dresses were draped over him. The evidence showed he had used an upside-down trash can to reach my clothes.

"What in the world are you doing?"

Unharmed, he held up a dress in each fist and announced, "Dis Papa's dress; dis Nana's dress! I go mailbox!"

I tumbled to the floor laughing and wrapped my arms around my silly little boy. He didn't understand my uncontrolled mirth or the tears cascading down my cheeks. But he embraced me wildly and kissed me, and together we laughed and laughed.

Later that evening, when it was quiet, I entered my invisible prayer closet. In a flash of clarity, I saw myself as a spiritual toddler. So often I am full of determination, pulling down my own answers to prayers, sure I understand what God means.

How ridiculous I must look!

Such realizations usually make me feel guilty, sad at having failed God, ashamed that I am so far from being what He wants me to be.

Not tonight, though.

Tonight my thoughts were of my son and how I'd embraced my fumbling toddler. How I'd laughed and how he had scrambled into my arms, freely receiving my love.

It suddenly seemed quite possible to me that my heavenly Father isn't disgusted or disappointed with me, after all. Maybe, as a loving parent, He watches me grow and delights in me simply because I am His child.

And maybe, just maybe, sometimes I make Him laugh.

And Sarah said,
"God has made me laugh,
so that all who hear
will laugh with me."

GENESIS 21:6 (NKJV)

Deep, Cleansing Breaths

Donna and I went shopping with our daughters today. Her Natalie is sixteen, my Rachel is eight. The excursion went something like this:

Natalie pulls a few bathing suits off the rack. Donna begins taking several deep, cleansing breaths which strangely resemble the breathing techniques we were taught in our childbirth classes years ago. We head for the dressing room. Rachel reaches for a few more swimsuits for Natalie to try on, and the two young ladies disappear behind the thick, blue curtain.

A few moments later, Rachel's round face appears. She asks if we want to see. Of course we do. Back goes the curtain, and there stands Natalie in a bathing suit that slides over her every curve. Donna holds her breath until Natalie says she doesn't like it. I hear Donna letting out a "hee, hee, hee, whew."

Natalie returns to the dressing room. I watch the clock. It's about three minutes between changes. Rachel pulls back the curtain and displays suit number two on her life-sized Barbie model. This one is a two-piece. Donna's breathing has turned noticeably more rapid.

Two minutes now between changes. We see suit number three, a rather

Donna begins taking several deep, cleansing breaths which strangely resemble the breathing techniques we were taught in our childbirth classes years ago.

"That's the one!"
Everyone is pleased.
We all congratulate
each other.
I pass around a roll
of Life Savers.

low-cut, black number. Donna begins sucking air in through clenched teeth. She seems a tad irritable, as if this transition is harder on her than it is on Natalie.

Here comes suit number four. Donna's face is red. She's clutching the sides of the chair and doesn't appear to be breathing at all. The curtain closes, and a stream of controlled breath passes through Donna's cracked lips. I consider going for ice chips, but it won't be long now, and I don't want to miss the Grand Conclusion. I coach Donna, telling her to hang in there. Just one more.

Rachel whips back the curtain, and Natalie turns around in number five, a lovely yet modest one-piece.

Donna's whole body pushes up from the chair, and with all her strength she announces, "That's the one!" Everyone is pleased. We all congratulate each other. I pass around a roll of Life Savers.

Thus I came to know and understand the real reason they teach us Lamaze. It has nothing to do with the infant in the delivery room. It's all about the teenage daughter in the dressing room.

MR. BOW TIE

When Young Ross was a year old, for Easter, I bought him a navy blue bow tie. The clasps didn't work, so I strung elastic through it, and he wore it as proud as could be with the elastic hidden under his button-down collar.

He loved that bow tie.

One afternoon that summer he found the tie in his dresser drawer and took it with him all over the house, carrying it between his teeth like a dogbone. When I put him down for his nap, I changed him into a dry T-shirt, took the soggy thing out of his mouth, and placed it on the dresser top. He snuggled right down.

About twenty minutes later I heard a strange noise out front. I left the pile of laundry on the kitchen table and opened the door.

There was my little nap boy, wide awake, riding his tricycle and wearing only (and I do mean only) a navy blue bow tie on an elastic string around his neck.

Can someone please tell me what this means?

Then our mouth
was filled with laughter,
and our tongue with singing.

PSALM 126:2 (NKJV)

FOR SPIKE'S SAKE

Young Ross begged to bring home one of the classroom guinea pigs at the end of his fourth-grade school year. We finally gave in, and "Spike" came to live in our garage. Everything went great until that winter when Rachel decided she needed a guinea pig, too—a girl guinea pig to keep Spike company in the garage on those snowy nights. We gave in again.

Daddy took her to the pet store and came home with a male—the pet store was fresh out of females. Rachel named him Bobby and introduced him to Spike with a gift of a new salt lick. Spike and Bobby seemed buddy-buddy enough, and life went on merrily until one day we noticed that Spike had gotten "fluffy."

Yes, Spike was really a Spikina, and of course Rachel was thrilled that Spikina was going to give us "a whole flock of babies." The men of the house were gone the weekend Spikina went into labor. We women brought fresh water, changed the newspaper in the cage, sent Bobby to a new bachelor pad (in the laundry bucket), and waited. And waited. And waited.

Rachel placed a chair in front of the cage where she sat for hours talking to Spikina, watching her pant and pant. I felt so helpless. What is normal delivery time for a guinea pig? How would I know if she was in distress? Were too many babies in there? Was one of them breach? Should I call a vet? How much would a vet charge for a house call to a guinea pig in labor?

Before I could force myself to make a decision about what to do for Spikina, she died.

Rachel cried.

I cried, too. We held each other, and Rachel said we must have a funeral. I was certain that was the least I could do. I pulled an empty Cap'n

Crunch box from the trash. We wrapped Spikina in blue floral paper towels and placed her in the cereal box. I took a shovel out to the side yard which faced the street that led to our cul-de-sac. There I began to dig a grave. The dry Nevada dirt proved rocky and unyielding. How did the pioneers ever forge a living from this earth? It was a huge effort to dig the hole. I wiped my brow.

Rachel emerged from the garden with a fistful of flowers. She asked me if guinea pigs have to live in cages in heaven or if they run free in the gardens.

I wasn't sure.

Together we placed Spikina and her unborn babies into the grave. I was about to shovel the dirt onto the cereal box when Rachel stopped me. She placed her daisies and petunias on top of the box and said, "Mother, we must sing."

Sing? What does one sing to a dead rodent in a Cap'n Crunch box?

Before I could come up with an appropriate hymn, Rachel cleared her throat, and on that hill, facing all our neighbors, she sang out clear and sweet, "As the guinea pig panteth for the water…"

YOU MAKE EACH DAY A MIRACLE

Today dawned like any other
and then "it" happened—
completely unexpectedly.
I saw in you, through you, with you
a glimmer of heaven.

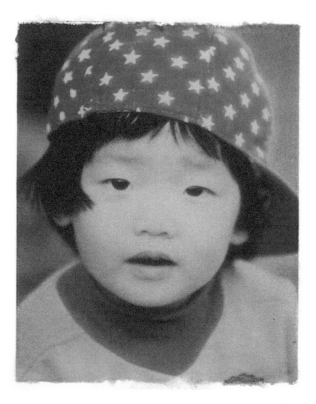

We will not hide them from their children,
Telling to the generation to come
The praises of the Lord,
And His strength
And His wonderful works that He has done.

PSALM 78:4 (NKJV)

THE FATHER'S PLEASURE

Today the wind invited the children and me outside to chase it. So we did. The trees, like dancing gypsies with jewels in their hair laughed above us as we frolicked down the street. The pockets of my jacket began to fill with autumn treasures, placed there by two sets of small hands.

Returning to the warm house, red-faced and breathless, the children dumped their goodies onto the kitchen table, giddy with the joy of discovery. Along with several twigs and many rocks, Young Ross had bagged a snail's shell—minus one snail. Rachel laid out each of her big, amber-colored leaves, then chose the largest one to use as a fan. I watched them as they arranged and rearranged each acorn, rock, leaf, and twig, preparing their own centerpiece for the table. The children spoke in hushed tones, lost in wonder, mesmerized by a handful of God's trinkets.

It reminded me of when I was young. I would regularly bring home treasures to my mother and scatter them across the kitchen counter. One afternoon her hand passed over the tiny white pebbles and squashed red geraniums extracted from my pockets to stop at a tattered gray feather. I had almost left the spiny thing in the gutter since it appeared broken and useless.

Mom ran her fingers up the feather's tattered sides and turned it toward the kitchen window. Soft hues of sunshine lit the feather, changing it from dull gray to bright silvery-blue as she twirled it between her fingers, a marvelous wonder to my young eyes. An "ordinary" miracle.

With fumbling words I entered my children's moment of wonder and told them how much God dearly treasured them. I wanted them to feel, in that moment, the pleasure of the Father, to understand how He delights in collecting the ordinary of this world and bringing it into the warmth of His kingdom. How his touch can turn the tattered into the dazzling.

Most of all, I wanted my children to know that their young hearts are not trinkets to be played with but are rare, priceless jewels in the hands of the King.

They looked at me with innocent eyes, non-plussed by my intense lecture. Had I once looked at my own mother the same way?

Maybe such eternal truths can't really be taught, I decided. They can only be collected, examined, arranged, rearranged—and finally treasured. And this takes a liftime of days filled with ordinary miracles.

Admonish the young women
to love their husbands, to love their children.

TITUS 2:4 (NKJV)

Swaying Hammock

There are a few exquisite moments
when life seems so full of joy and wonder that its seams
nearly burst with goodness.

I feel that way today. I'm not sure why.

I love my husband.
I love my children.

I love this house.
I love the blossoming apple tree in the backyard.
I love this tablecloth.
I love the sound of the cows' bells on the hill.
I love the swaying hammock bidding me
to surrender to its caress.

I love that I don't know what tomorrow will bring.
But I know the One who will bring it effortlessly
on the morning winds.

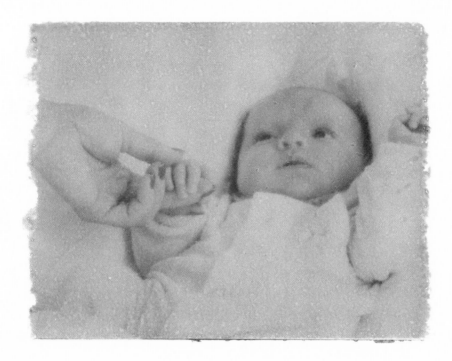

Her Hands

My mother's hands are cool and fair,
They can do anything.
Delicate mercies hide them there
Like flowers in the spring.

When I was small and could not sleep,
She used to come to me,
And with my cheek upon her hand
How sure my rest would be.

For everything she ever touched
Of beautiful or fine,
Their memories living in her hands
Would warm that sleep of mine.

Her hands remember how they played
One time in meadow streams,

And all the flickering song and shade
Of water took my dreams.

Swift through her haunted fingers pass
Memories of garden things;
Dipped my face in flowers and grass
And sounds of hidden wings.

One time she touched the cloud that kissed
Brown pastures bleak and far;
I leaned my cheek into a mist
And thought it was a star.

All this was very long ago
And I am grown; but yet
The hand that lured my slumber so
I never can forget.

ANNA HEMPSTEAD BRANCH

My Five-Year-Old Warrior

I watch my five-year-old lower himself into the steaming tub where Mr. Bubble ministers to the wounds my son has suffered in battle today.

His arms bear scratches from the apple tree he scaled, and both knees are streaked with bloody reminders of his encounter with the sidewalk while charging on his trusty Huffy.

Gently I towel down his bruised thighs, dotted with bites from relentless mosquitoes.

With vigor I rough up his sun-bleached hair and shoo him into his room where he dresses himself for bed.

A story, a prayer, a hug, and a kiss.

My brave warrior closes his eyes, and I stand back, marveling that this long, sturdy body, lying lumpy beneath the covers, once fit in my arms and nursed at my breast.

Many summer nights, just like this one, I rocked him. For hours I rocked and I sang and I prayed. Oh, how I prayed!

I close his door softly. My soldier needs his sleep.

Tomorrow great battles will be fought...in the sandbox, on his skateboard, with the neighborhood kids. He will return to me, bloodied and bruised, and there will be so little I can do. I have no power over scraped knees and stubbed toes.

But the real battle—the one not against flesh and blood but against principalities and powers of the air—has already begun in his young life.

And in that battle, I am the warrior.

I pray.

Oh, how I pray!

That God will have the ultimate victory.

*Never be afraid to trust
an unknown future to a known God.*

CORRIE TEN BOOM

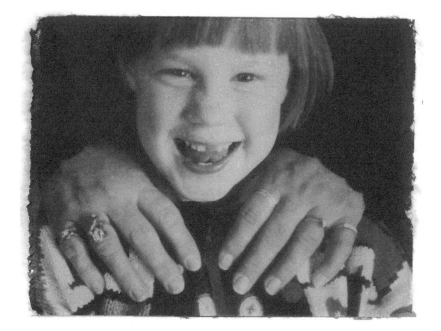

Expect resistance but pray for miracles.

CORRIE TEN BOOM

The Wish beneath My Pillow

The kids were both at school today when I found my wish. I was cleaning closets and discovered a small, unmarked box on my son's top shelf. I placed it on the edge of the bed. It toppled over, spilling its contents onto the floor. The first thing I saw was a tiny blue tennis shoe. "His first pair of running Nikes" my brother had written on the gift card. I picked up the unbelievably small shoe and held it in the palm of my hand. I couldn't help but compare. Reaching inside the closet, I extracted one smelly high-top tennis shoe, big boy's size two. I held them next to each other. The contrast was mind-boggling.

That night I looked at my nine-year-old's feet as he came to the dinner table. I stared at them tucked under the table as he did his homework. I watched him walk up the stairs. When I tucked him in bed, I grabbed his right foot and gave it a playful wrangle. It no longer fit in the palm of my hand.

After the kids were asleep, I slipped upstairs and retrieved the baby shoe I'd hidden among my socks that afternoon. Nobody saw me press the silly little thing to my cheek and then tuck it under my pillow.

Ross and I went to bed several hours later. I curled up next to my warm husband and slipped my hand between the cool sheets and my pillowcase. It was still there. I clutched the tiny shoe, closed my eyes, held my breath, and made a wish.

What did I wish? I'll never tell. But it might have something to do with a pair of feet that could fit in these shoes.

Nobody saw me press the silly little thing to my cheek and then tuck it under my pillow.

WORKING MOM

"I have written more than anybody...would have thought. I have taught an hour a day in our school, and I have read two hours every evening to the children.... Since I began this note I have been called off at least a dozen times—once to buy codfish from the fisherman; once to see a man who had brought me some barrels of apples; once to see a bookman; then to Mrs. Upman to see about a drawing I promised to make for her; then to nurse the baby; then into the kitchen to make chowder for dinner; and now I'm at it again, for nothing but deadly determination enables me ever to write; it is rowing against wind and tide."

HARRIET BEECHER STOWE

MOMENT BY MOMENT

We went to a barbecue today at the Kimber Park Pool. It was a gorgeous, hot Sunday afternoon. Sally and I stood by the picnic tables with our arms around each other, our warm cheeks pressed close, smiling as we posed and waited for Al to figure out why the camera wouldn't snap our picture.

There was a sudden commotion at the pool, thirty feet from where we stood. The lifeguard was pulling up a toddler. It was my Rachel!

I raced to the pool, incredulous that she could have moved that fast in such short time. She had been clutching my leg all afternoon. When did she let go? Why didn't I realize it?

The lifeguard handed her to me. Her little pink Sunday dress dripped pool water down my leg. I held her close as she coughed and coughed and then wailed with all the force of her twenty-month-old lungs. Everyone gathered around. She cried and cried and spit up her watermelon and Ritz crackers. I sat down in a lounge chair where she clung to me and whimpered. I wrapped her in a towel, and she fell asleep. When she woke up, she was all smiles and wanted me to push her on the swing.

It's now past two in the morning, and I can't sleep. Why didn't anyone tell me about this feeling? How many more times will this scene play itself over in my mind? When does it go away?

Forget everything anyone ever told me about how to be a good mother! I am at the mercy of a living, breathing God. He is the giver, sustainer, and taker of life.

Today He gave.

Mothers for miles around
worried about Zuckerman's swing.
They feared some child would fall off.
But no child ever did.
Children almost always hang onto things
tighter than their parents
think they will.

E. B. WHITE
CHARLOTTE'S WEB

DIDN'T YOU GROW TOO FAST?

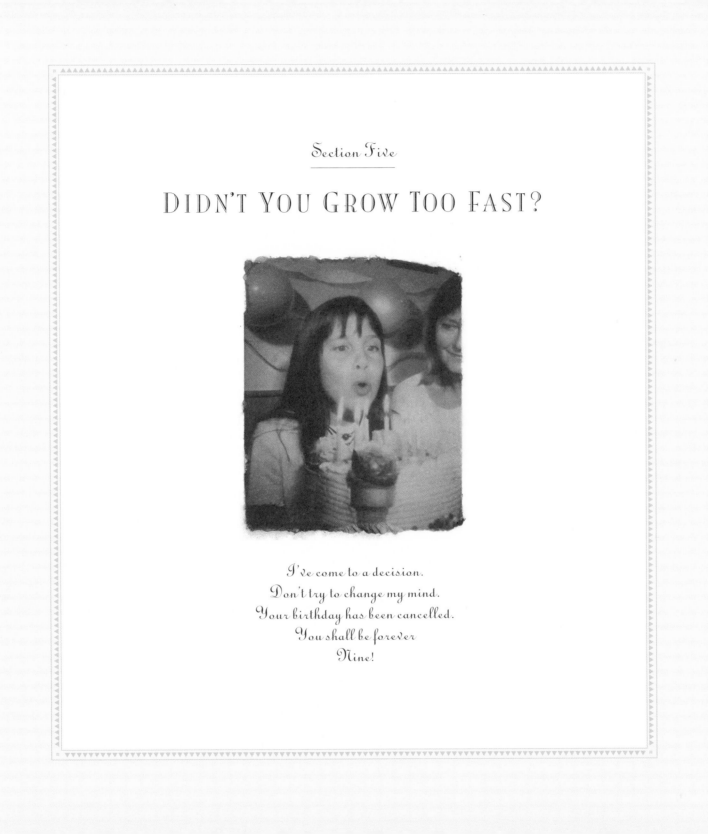

I've come to a decision.
Don't try to change my mind.
Your birthday has been cancelled.
You shall be forever
Nine!

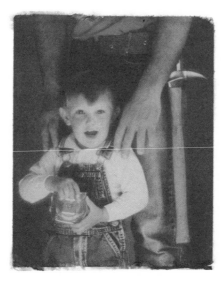

My son, give attention to my words;
Incline your ear to my sayings.

Do not let them depart from your eyes;
Keep them in the midst of your heart;

For they are life to those who find them,
And health to all their flesh.

Keep your heart with all diligence,
For out of it spring the issues of life.

PROVERBS 4:20-23 (NKJV)

HOLDING BACK TIME

The kids and I went up to the lake today, eager to escape the heat. We settled in the sand at Kings Beach, and off Rachel and Young Ross ran to play in the water.

I heard some girls giggling and scanned the shoreline until I saw the three bikini-clad junior high girls splashing water at a boy and running before he could splash them back. Of course they returned for more splashes and more carefree giggling.

Ah, youth!

Under the August sun I wiggled my toes into the sand and thought back on my wonder years when my sister and I spent our summers innocently flirting with the boys at the beach. We were just like those girls, all arms and legs, chasing boys. Teasing them. Diligently planning our attacks until we got one of them to respond.

I smiled at those adorably skinny girls, feeling a sense of sisterhood. Of camaraderie. I marveled at the timeless elixir of sand, sun, and shore. Of how it is mixed vigorously by the summer wind and poured out on innocents, whisking them from childhood to adulthood. I watched as the skipping, giggling girls honed in on their unsuspecting victim and...

Suddenly I sprang from my chair.

Those girls weren't flirting with boys! They were chasing my boy, my baby! Why those..., those...hussies! How dare they? You little flirts! Get away from him! Do you hear me? Shoo! Go away!

Certainly my son would not respond to such immature antics.

But he was.

He was splashing them back, smiling and looking manly with his chest all puffed out and his hands on his hips. The summer wind was shame-lessly at work, right before my eyes, enticing my boy into puberty. He shouldn't respond yet, should he? He's only eleven.

Eleven?

Eleven!

When did he turn eleven?

I shielded my eyes from the sun with my arm and continued to stare. I refused to blink. I didn't dare. I knew if I closed my eyes for even one sec-ond, my baby boy would suddenly be transformed into a man.

Like Mother, Like Daughter

R achel came home from school today with Kristin's phone number—memorized! This is a first. I watch her march to the portable phone and say the number aloud as she dials. "Hello. This is Rachel Gunn. May I please speak to Kristin?"

She balances the phone on her shoulder, just the way I do, and begins to walk around the house. I don't look like that, do I?

"Hi, Kristin. It's Rachel." She opens the cupboard and checks for snacks, still balancing the phone.

"Nothing. What are you doing?"

She heads for the front porch with a handful of pretzels.

I call out after her, "Would you like something to drink?"

She half turns and, with a sweet facial expression and a finger touched to her lips, silently motions for me not to interrupt her. Is that what I do?

I casually follow her to the porch and nestle on the wicker love seat. I begin flipping through a magazine. Rachel's eyes meet mine, and she gives me a "don't you have anything better to do than follow me around all day?" look.

She speaks. Not to me, but to that invisible person on the phone. "I remembered your number."

Rachel's eyes meet mine, and she gives me a "don't you have anything better to do than follow me around all day?" look.

"Do you
know that I think
you're absolutely
amazing?"

She checks the hanging petunias with her free hand to see if they need water. There she is, balancing the phone on her shoulder, clutching pretzels with her right hand, and fingering the soil with her left. Just like her mother.

"Well, that's all. I guess I'll see you tomorrow at school."

She wipes her muddy finger on a leaf, still balancing the phone. Then clutching her wad of pretzels, she pulls a wicker chair toward her with her foot—just like I do.

"Okay. Bye."

I watch as Rachel pulls the phone away from her ear with her free hand, then catches a pretzel between her teeth and presses the "off" button with her nose. Just like . . .

"Do you know what?" I tell her as she joins me on the love seat and tries to fit her pre-adolescent body onto my lap. "Do you know that I think you're absolutely amazing?"

She smiles, kisses me on the tip of my nose, and says, "I know. That's 'cause I'm just like you."

What a Mother Says

Oh, let me hold her!

How's my little angel?

Hush, baby girl.

Aren't you sleepy yet?

It's okay. Don't cry.

No, no. Don't touch.

Come to Mommy.

Take that out of your mouth. Yucky!

That's not for you.

You don't need that anymore.

You're a big girl now.

Tell Mommy if you need to go potty, okay?

Don't get into your brother's things.

Go to your room.

No, you may not.

I just brought you a drink of water.

Get back in bed.

Pick up your toys.

Don't play inside the clothes rack.

Can you draw a picture for Grandma?

Hold still.

Can you remember to bring it home tomorrow?

I'm sure she still wants to be your friend.

Did you practice?

Try looking under your bed.

Go wash your hands.

You're not old enough yet.

You'll have to ask your father.

Where was it when you last saw it?

Stop teasing your brother.

Go clean your room. Come set the table.

Don't bite your nails.

Did you do your homework?

Get off the phone. Eat your vegetables.

You're responsible to keep track of your own things.

Did you tell me it was this Saturday?

Sure——if you want to use your own money.

Tell her you'll call her back.

Try on a bigger size.

There's a boy on the phone for you.

You may not wear that to school.

Be back by your curfew.

I did not say it was okay.

Come straight home.

No, I need the car this afternoon.

Are you coming home this weekend? Next weekend?

What do you know about him?

Have you thought this through?

I ordered them because I thought you'd appreciate them.

But pink used to be your favorite color.

Whatever you want. It's up to you.

Don't sit on your veil.

Call us when you get there. Don't slip on the rice.

Good-bye, honey.

MOTHER MINE

A mother's heart holds many charms

And love is ever in her arms.

And in her eyes a faith divine.

And home is you,

Mother Mine.

WHAT A MOTHER THINKS

I love you so much.

There is no way I can possibly put into words how proud I am of you.

You're absolutely beautiful.

Sometimes when our eyes meet,

it's like gazing into a reflecting pool.

I see in you glimmers of my past.

Do you see in me hints of your future?

You are everything I ever prayed for.

There's nothing about you I'd change.

I love you more than you will ever know,

more than you will ever ask.

There's nothing I wouldn't give for you,

nothing I wouldn't do for you.

You are my daughter,

and I will always love you

with a love so immense

so eternal

I could never find a way to squeeze it into words.

WHAT A DAUGHTER THINKS

My mother doesn't understand me.
She never has,
and she never will.

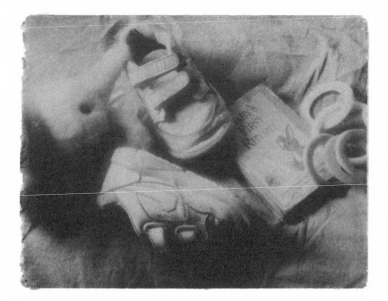

View from My Window

I'm home from the hospital. What a harrowing week.

The tumor was benign. I am "repaired."

Dozens of ugly silver staples bind my flesh together.

Outside the trees are beginning to bud. The lawns are all green.

Fat pigeons strut on the roof of Sandra's yellow house.

A perky little squirrel keeps stopping by my second-story window.

He raises his paws and presses his nose to the glass.

He sits and watches, like a child peering through the window of a toy store.

What does he see? The many bouquets?

The basket of cards from my well-wishing friends?

The whirling ceiling fan? This pale woman propped up watching him?

Oh, here he is now! Hello, my furry friend.

He's scratching at the glass, looking this way and that.

On the phone lines behind him, four pigeons perform their high wire act.

All they need are tiny parasols.

And maybe a roasted nut cart to entice my fluffy-tailed friend

to stop watching me and start watching them.

A jogger in a purple shirt huffs by,

startling the acrobats and sending them across the street to Sandra's roof

where six of them now strut and coo.

It's a busy world out there. So very busy. So full of life.

In here?

I close my eyes to sleep. To quiet my soul. To heal.

Yes, the danger is passed. I am repaired.

And I shall never have another child.

At thirty-nine such news shouldn't shock me.

A friend said I should feel relieved.

But for so many years I've wondered if perhaps

there might be one more tiny life within me, waiting to be born.

Now it's evident the answer is no.

What are you staring at, Mr. Squirrel?

Have you never seen a mother's tears?

SWEET DREAMS

Trade winds dancing with the palm trees,
Turquoise waves rushing to kiss the shore,
A fat, yellow moon winking at me,
Sweet baby asleep in my arms—
There is nothing else in the entire world
that I desire.